BABY'S NAME

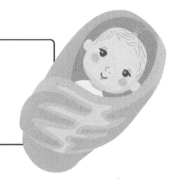

NOTES & IMPORTANT CONTACTS

📅 DATE	#️⃣ WEEK	⚖️ WEIGHT

FEED

MEALS	AMOUNT	TIME

SLEEP

FROM	TO	DURATION

ACTIVITIES

DESCRIPTION	DURATION

DIAPER CHANGES

TIME	RESULT
	WET / BM
	WET / BM
	WET / BM
	WET / BM
	WET / BM
	WET / BM
	WET / BM
	WET / BM

SHOPPING LIST

- ○
- ○
- ○
- ○
- ○

SPECIAL CARE

DATE	WEEK	⚖ WEIGHT

FEED

MEALS	AMOUNT	TIME

SLEEP

FROM	TO	DURATION

ACTIVITIES

DESCRIPTION	DURATION

DIAPER CHANGES

TIME	RESULT
	WET / BM
	WET / BM
	WET / BM
	WET / BM
	WET / BM
	WET / BM
	WET / BM
	WET / BM

SHOPPING LIST

- ◯
- ◯
- ◯
- ◯
- ◯

SPECIAL CARE

📅 DATE	# WEEK	⚖️ WEIGHT

FEED

MEALS	AMOUNT	TIME

SLEEP

FROM	TO	DURATION

ACTIVITIES

DESCRIPTION	DURATION

DIAPER CHANGES

TIME	RESULT
	WET / BM
	WET / BM
	WET / BM
	WET / BM
	WET / BM
	WET / BM
	WET / BM
	WET / BM

SHOPPING LIST

- ○
- ○
- ○
- ○
- ○

SPECIAL CARE

📅 DATE	# WEEK	⚖ WEIGHT

FEED

MEALS	AMOUNT	TIME

SLEEP

FROM	TO	DURATION

ACTIVITIES

DESCRIPTION	DURATION

DIAPER CHANGES

TIME	RESULT
	WET / BM
	WET / BM
	WET / BM
	WET / BM
	WET / BM
	WET / BM
	WET / BM
	WET / BM

SHOPPING LIST

- ◯
- ◯
- ◯
- ◯
- ◯

SPECIAL CARE

📅 DATE	#️⃣ WEEK	⚖️ WEIGHT

FEED

MEALS	AMOUNT	TIME

SLEEP

FROM	TO	DURATION

ACTIVITIES

DESCRIPTION	DURATION

DIAPER CHANGES

TIME	RESULT
	WET / BM
	WET / BM
	WET / BM
	WET / BM
	WET / BM
	WET / BM
	WET / BM
	WET / BM

SHOPPING LIST

- ○
- ○
- ○
- ○
- ○

SPECIAL CARE

📅 DATE	#️⃣ WEEK	⚖️ WEIGHT

FEED

MEALS	AMOUNT	TIME

SLEEP

FROM	TO	DURATION

ACTIVITIES

DESCRIPTION	DURATION

DIAPER CHANGES

TIME	RESULT
	WET / BM
	WET / BM
	WET / BM
	WET / BM
	WET / BM
	WET / BM
	WET / BM
	WET / BM

SHOPPING LIST

- ◯
- ◯
- ◯
- ◯
- ◯

SPECIAL CARE

🗓 DATE	#️⃣ WEEK	⚖️ WEIGHT

FEED

MEALS	AMOUNT	TIME

SLEEP

FROM	TO	DURATION

ACTIVITIES

DESCRIPTION	DURATION

DIAPER CHANGES

TIME	RESULT
	WET / BM
	WET / BM
	WET / BM
	WET / BM
	WET / BM
	WET / BM
	WET / BM
	WET / BM

SHOPPING LIST

- ◯
- ◯
- ◯
- ◯
- ◯

SPECIAL CARE

DATE	WEEK	🪣 WEIGHT

FEED

MEALS	AMOUNT	TIME

SLEEP

FROM	TO	DURATION

ACTIVITIES

DESCRIPTION	DURATION

DIAPER CHANGES

TIME	RESULT
	WET / BM
	WET / BM
	WET / BM
	WET / BM
	WET / BM
	WET / BM
	WET / BM
	WET / BM

SHOPPING LIST

- ◯
- ◯
- ◯
- ◯
- ◯

SPECIAL CARE

📅 DATE	#️⃣ WEEK	⚖️ WEIGHT

FEED		
MEALS	AMOUNT	TIME

SLEEP		
FROM	TO	DURATION

ACTIVITIES	
DESCRIPTION	DURATION

DIAPER CHANGES	
TIME	RESULT
	WET / BM
	WET / BM
	WET / BM
	WET / BM
	WET / BM
	WET / BM
	WET / BM
	WET / BM

SHOPPING LIST
○
○
○
○
○

SPECIAL CARE

📅 DATE	# WEEK	⚖ WEIGHT

FEED

MEALS	AMOUNT	TIME

SLEEP

FROM	TO	DURATION

ACTIVITIES

DESCRIPTION	DURATION

DIAPER CHANGES

TIME	RESULT
	WET / BM
	WET / BM
	WET / BM
	WET / BM
	WET / BM
	WET / BM
	WET / BM
	WET / BM

SHOPPING LIST

- ○
- ○
- ○
- ○
- ○

SPECIAL CARE

DATE	WEEK	WEIGHT

FEED

MEALS	AMOUNT	TIME

SLEEP

FROM	TO	DURATION

ACTIVITIES

DESCRIPTION	DURATION

DIAPER CHANGES

TIME	RESULT
	WET / BM
	WET / BM
	WET / BM
	WET / BM
	WET / BM
	WET / BM
	WET / BM
	WET / BM

SHOPPING LIST

- ○
- ○
- ○
- ○
- ○

SPECIAL CARE

📅 DATE	#️⃣ WEEK	⚖️ WEIGHT

FEED

MEALS	AMOUNT	TIME

SLEEP

FROM	TO	DURATION

ACTIVITIES

DESCRIPTION	DURATION

DIAPER CHANGES

TIME	RESULT
	WET / BM
	WET / BM
	WET / BM
	WET / BM
	WET / BM
	WET / BM
	WET / BM
	WET / BM

SHOPPING LIST

- ◯
- ◯
- ◯
- ◯
- ◯

SPECIAL CARE

📅 DATE	#️⃣ WEEK	⚖️ WEIGHT

FEED		
MEALS	AMOUNT	TIME

SLEEP		
FROM	TO	DURATION

ACTIVITIES	
DESCRIPTION	DURATION

DIAPER CHANGES	
TIME	RESULT
	WET / BM
	WET / BM
	WET / BM
	WET / BM
	WET / BM
	WET / BM
	WET / BM
	WET / BM

SHOPPING LIST
◯
◯
◯
◯
◯

SPECIAL CARE

📅 DATE	# WEEK	⚖️ WEIGHT

FEED

MEALS	AMOUNT	TIME

SLEEP

FROM	TO	DURATION

ACTIVITIES

DESCRIPTION	DURATION

DIAPER CHANGES

TIME	RESULT
	WET / BM
	WET / BM
	WET / BM
	WET / BM
	WET / BM
	WET / BM
	WET / BM
	WET / BM

SHOPPING LIST

- ○
- ○
- ○
- ○
- ○

SPECIAL CARE

📅 DATE	# WEEK	⚖️ WEIGHT

FEED

MEALS	AMOUNT	TIME

SLEEP

FROM	TO	DURATION

ACTIVITIES

DESCRIPTION	DURATION

DIAPER CHANGES

TIME	RESULT
	WET / BM
	WET / BM
	WET / BM
	WET / BM
	WET / BM
	WET / BM
	WET / BM
	WET / BM

SHOPPING LIST

- ◯
- ◯
- ◯
- ◯
- ◯

SPECIAL CARE

📅 DATE	# WEEK	⚖ WEIGHT

FEED

MEALS	AMOUNT	TIME

SLEEP

FROM	TO	DURATION

ACTIVITIES

DESCRIPTION	DURATION

DIAPER CHANGES

TIME	RESULT
	WET / BM
	WET / BM
	WET / BM
	WET / BM
	WET / BM
	WET / BM
	WET / BM
	WET / BM

SHOPPING LIST

- ◯
- ◯
- ◯
- ◯
- ◯

SPECIAL CARE

📅 DATE	#️⃣ WEEK	⚖️ WEIGHT

FEED		
MEALS	AMOUNT	TIME

SLEEP		
FROM	TO	DURATION

ACTIVITIES	
DESCRIPTION	DURATION

DIAPER CHANGES	
TIME	RESULT
	WET / BM
	WET / BM
	WET / BM
	WET / BM
	WET / BM
	WET / BM
	WET / BM
	WET / BM

SHOPPING LIST
◯
◯
◯
◯
◯

SPECIAL CARE

📅 DATE	#️⃣ WEEK	⚖️ WEIGHT

FEED

MEALS	AMOUNT	TIME

SLEEP

FROM	TO	DURATION

ACTIVITIES

DESCRIPTION	DURATION

DIAPER CHANGES

TIME	RESULT
	WET / BM
	WET / BM
	WET / BM
	WET / BM
	WET / BM
	WET / BM
	WET / BM
	WET / BM

SHOPPING LIST

- ◯
- ◯
- ◯
- ◯
- ◯

SPECIAL CARE

📅 DATE	#️⃣ WEEK	⚖️ WEIGHT

FEED

MEALS	AMOUNT	TIME

SLEEP

FROM	TO	DURATION

ACTIVITIES

DESCRIPTION	DURATION

DIAPER CHANGES

TIME	RESULT
	WET / BM
	WET / BM
	WET / BM
	WET / BM
	WET / BM
	WET / BM
	WET / BM
	WET / BM

SHOPPING LIST

- ○
- ○
- ○
- ○
- ○

SPECIAL CARE

📅 DATE	# WEEK	⚖️ WEIGHT

FEED

MEALS	AMOUNT	TIME

SLEEP

FROM	TO	DURATION

ACTIVITIES

DESCRIPTION	DURATION

DIAPER CHANGES

TIME	RESULT
	WET / BM
	WET / BM
	WET / BM
	WET / BM
	WET / BM
	WET / BM
	WET / BM
	WET / BM

SHOPPING LIST

- ○
- ○
- ○
- ○
- ○

SPECIAL CARE

📅 DATE	#️⃣ WEEK	⚖️ WEIGHT

FEED

MEALS	AMOUNT	TIME

SLEEP

FROM	TO	DURATION

ACTIVITIES

DESCRIPTION	DURATION

DIAPER CHANGES

TIME	RESULT
	WET / BM
	WET / BM
	WET / BM
	WET / BM
	WET / BM
	WET / BM
	WET / BM
	WET / BM

SHOPPING LIST

- ○
- ○
- ○
- ○
- ○

SPECIAL CARE

📅 DATE	# WEEK	⚖ WEIGHT

FEED

MEALS	AMOUNT	TIME

SLEEP

FROM	TO	DURATION

ACTIVITIES

DESCRIPTION	DURATION

DIAPER CHANGES

TIME	RESULT
	WET / BM
	WET / BM
	WET / BM
	WET / BM
	WET / BM
	WET / BM
	WET / BM
	WET / BM

SHOPPING LIST

- ○
- ○
- ○
- ○
- ○

SPECIAL CARE

📅 DATE	#️⃣ WEEK	⚖️ WEIGHT

FEED		
MEALS	AMOUNT	TIME

SLEEP		
FROM	TO	DURATION

ACTIVITIES	
DESCRIPTION	DURATION

DIAPER CHANGES	
TIME	RESULT
	WET / BM
	WET / BM
	WET / BM
	WET / BM
	WET / BM
	WET / BM
	WET / BM
	WET / BM

SHOPPING LIST
◯
◯
◯
◯
◯

SPECIAL CARE

📅 DATE	#️⃣ WEEK	⚖️ WEIGHT

FEED

MEALS	AMOUNT	TIME

SLEEP

FROM	TO	DURATION

ACTIVITIES

DESCRIPTION	DURATION

DIAPER CHANGES

TIME	RESULT
	WET / BM
	WET / BM
	WET / BM
	WET / BM
	WET / BM
	WET / BM
	WET / BM
	WET / BM

SHOPPING LIST

- ◯
- ◯
- ◯
- ◯
- ◯

SPECIAL CARE

📅 DATE	#️⃣ WEEK	⚖️ WEIGHT

FEED

MEALS	AMOUNT	TIME

SLEEP

FROM	TO	DURATION

ACTIVITIES

DESCRIPTION	DURATION

DIAPER CHANGES

TIME	RESULT
	WET / BM
	WET / BM
	WET / BM
	WET / BM
	WET / BM
	WET / BM
	WET / BM
	WET / BM

SHOPPING LIST

○
○
○
○
○

SPECIAL CARE

📅 DATE	#️⃣ WEEK	⚖️ WEIGHT

FEED

MEALS	AMOUNT	TIME

SLEEP

FROM	TO	DURATION

ACTIVITIES

DESCRIPTION	DURATION

DIAPER CHANGES

TIME	RESULT
	WET / BM
	WET / BM
	WET / BM
	WET / BM
	WET / BM
	WET / BM
	WET / BM
	WET / BM

SHOPPING LIST

- ○
- ○
- ○
- ○
- ○

SPECIAL CARE

🗓 DATE	# WEEK	⚖ WEIGHT

FEED

MEALS	AMOUNT	TIME

SLEEP

FROM	TO	DURATION

ACTIVITIES

DESCRIPTION	DURATION

DIAPER CHANGES

TIME	RESULT
	WET / BM
	WET / BM
	WET / BM
	WET / BM
	WET / BM
	WET / BM
	WET / BM
	WET / BM

SHOPPING LIST

- ◯
- ◯
- ◯
- ◯
- ◯

SPECIAL CARE

📅 DATE	# WEEK	⚖️ WEIGHT

FEED

MEALS	AMOUNT	TIME

SLEEP

FROM	TO	DURATION

ACTIVITIES

DESCRIPTION	DURATION

DIAPER CHANGES

TIME	RESULT
	WET / BM
	WET / BM
	WET / BM
	WET / BM
	WET / BM
	WET / BM
	WET / BM
	WET / BM

SHOPPING LIST

- ○
- ○
- ○
- ○
- ○

SPECIAL CARE

📅 DATE	# WEEK	⚖️ WEIGHT

FEED		
MEALS	AMOUNT	TIME

SLEEP		
FROM	TO	DURATION

ACTIVITIES	
DESCRIPTION	DURATION

DIAPER CHANGES	
TIME	RESULT
	WET / BM
	WET / BM
	WET / BM
	WET / BM
	WET / BM
	WET / BM
	WET / BM
	WET / BM

SHOPPING LIST
○
○
○
○
○

SPECIAL CARE

📅 DATE	#️⃣ WEEK	⚖️ WEIGHT

FEED

MEALS	AMOUNT	TIME

SLEEP

FROM	TO	DURATION

ACTIVITIES

DESCRIPTION	DURATION

DIAPER CHANGES

TIME	RESULT
	WET / BM
	WET / BM
	WET / BM
	WET / BM
	WET / BM
	WET / BM
	WET / BM
	WET / BM

SHOPPING LIST

- ◯
- ◯
- ◯
- ◯
- ◯

SPECIAL CARE

📅 DATE	#️ WEEK	⚖️ WEIGHT

FEED

MEALS	AMOUNT	TIME

SLEEP

FROM	TO	DURATION

ACTIVITIES

DESCRIPTION	DURATION

DIAPER CHANGES

TIME	RESULT
	WET / BM
	WET / BM
	WET / BM
	WET / BM
	WET / BM
	WET / BM
	WET / BM
	WET / BM

SHOPPING LIST

- ◯
- ◯
- ◯
- ◯
- ◯

SPECIAL CARE

📅 DATE	# WEEK	⚖️ WEIGHT

FEED

MEALS	AMOUNT	TIME

SLEEP

FROM	TO	DURATION

ACTIVITIES

DESCRIPTION	DURATION

DIAPER CHANGES

TIME	RESULT
	WET / BM
	WET / BM
	WET / BM
	WET / BM
	WET / BM
	WET / BM
	WET / BM
	WET / BM

SHOPPING LIST

- ◯
- ◯
- ◯
- ◯
- ◯

SPECIAL CARE

📅 DATE	# WEEK	⚖ WEIGHT

FEED

MEALS	AMOUNT	TIME

SLEEP

FROM	TO	DURATION

ACTIVITIES

DESCRIPTION	DURATION

DIAPER CHANGES

TIME	RESULT
	WET / BM
	WET / BM
	WET / BM
	WET / BM
	WET / BM
	WET / BM
	WET / BM
	WET / BM

SHOPPING LIST

- ◯
- ◯
- ◯
- ◯
- ◯

SPECIAL CARE

DATE	# WEEK	WEIGHT

FEED

MEALS	AMOUNT	TIME

SLEEP

FROM	TO	DURATION

ACTIVITIES

DESCRIPTION	DURATION

DIAPER CHANGES

TIME	RESULT
	WET / BM
	WET / BM
	WET / BM
	WET / BM
	WET / BM
	WET / BM
	WET / BM
	WET / BM

SHOPPING LIST

- ◯
- ◯
- ◯
- ◯
- ◯

SPECIAL CARE

📅 DATE	#️⃣ WEEK	⚖️ WEIGHT

FEED				SLEEP		
MEALS	AMOUNT	TIME		FROM	TO	DURATION

ACTIVITIES			DIAPER CHANGES	
DESCRIPTION	DURATION		TIME	RESULT
				WET / BM
				WET / BM
				WET / BM
				WET / BM
				WET / BM
				WET / BM
				WET / BM
				WET / BM

SHOPPING LIST	SPECIAL CARE
◯	
◯	
◯	
◯	
◯	

📅 DATE	# WEEK	⚖️ WEIGHT

FEED

MEALS	AMOUNT	TIME

SLEEP

FROM	TO	DURATION

ACTIVITIES

DESCRIPTION	DURATION

DIAPER CHANGES

TIME	RESULT
	WET / BM
	WET / BM
	WET / BM
	WET / BM
	WET / BM
	WET / BM
	WET / BM
	WET / BM

SHOPPING LIST

- ○
- ○
- ○
- ○
- ○

SPECIAL CARE

📅 DATE	#️⃣ WEEK	⚖️ WEIGHT

FEED

MEALS	AMOUNT	TIME

SLEEP

FROM	TO	DURATION

ACTIVITIES

DESCRIPTION	DURATION

DIAPER CHANGES

TIME	RESULT
	WET / BM
	WET / BM
	WET / BM
	WET / BM
	WET / BM
	WET / BM
	WET / BM
	WET / BM

SHOPPING LIST

- ◯
- ◯
- ◯
- ◯
- ◯

SPECIAL CARE

📅 DATE	# WEEK	⚖️ WEIGHT

FEED

MEALS	AMOUNT	TIME

SLEEP

FROM	TO	DURATION

ACTIVITIES

DESCRIPTION	DURATION

DIAPER CHANGES

TIME	RESULT
	WET / BM
	WET / BM
	WET / BM
	WET / BM
	WET / BM
	WET / BM
	WET / BM
	WET / BM

SHOPPING LIST

- ◯
- ◯
- ◯
- ◯
- ◯

SPECIAL CARE

📅 DATE	#️⃣ WEEK	⚖️ WEIGHT

FEED

MEALS	AMOUNT	TIME

SLEEP

FROM	TO	DURATION

ACTIVITIES

DESCRIPTION	DURATION

DIAPER CHANGES

TIME	RESULT
	WET / BM
	WET / BM
	WET / BM
	WET / BM
	WET / BM
	WET / BM
	WET / BM
	WET / BM

SHOPPING LIST

- ○
- ○
- ○
- ○
- ○

SPECIAL CARE

📅 DATE	#️⃣ WEEK	⚖️ WEIGHT

FEED

MEALS	AMOUNT	TIME

SLEEP

FROM	TO	DURATION

ACTIVITIES

DESCRIPTION	DURATION

DIAPER CHANGES

TIME	RESULT
	WET / BM
	WET / BM
	WET / BM
	WET / BM
	WET / BM
	WET / BM
	WET / BM
	WET / BM

SHOPPING LIST

- ◯
- ◯
- ◯
- ◯
- ◯

SPECIAL CARE

📅 DATE	#️⃣ WEEK	⚖️ WEIGHT

FEED		
MEALS	AMOUNT	TIME

SLEEP		
FROM	TO	DURATION

ACTIVITIES	
DESCRIPTION	DURATION

DIAPER CHANGES	
TIME	RESULT
	WET / BM
	WET / BM
	WET / BM
	WET / BM
	WET / BM
	WET / BM
	WET / BM
	WET / BM

SHOPPING LIST
◯
◯
◯
◯
◯

SPECIAL CARE

📅 DATE	# WEEK	⚖️ WEIGHT

FEED

MEALS	AMOUNT	TIME

SLEEP

FROM	TO	DURATION

ACTIVITIES

DESCRIPTION	DURATION

DIAPER CHANGES

TIME	RESULT
	WET / BM
	WET / BM
	WET / BM
	WET / BM
	WET / BM
	WET / BM
	WET / BM
	WET / BM

SHOPPING LIST

- ○
- ○
- ○
- ○
- ○

SPECIAL CARE

DATE	WEEK	WEIGHT

FEED

MEALS	AMOUNT	TIME

SLEEP

FROM	TO	DURATION

ACTIVITIES

DESCRIPTION	DURATION

DIAPER CHANGES

TIME	RESULT
	WET / BM
	WET / BM
	WET / BM
	WET / BM
	WET / BM
	WET / BM
	WET / BM
	WET / BM

SHOPPING LIST

- ○
- ○
- ○
- ○
- ○

SPECIAL CARE

📅 DATE	# WEEK	⚖ WEIGHT

FEED

MEALS	AMOUNT	TIME

SLEEP

FROM	TO	DURATION

ACTIVITIES

DESCRIPTION	DURATION

DIAPER CHANGES

TIME	RESULT
	WET / BM
	WET / BM
	WET / BM
	WET / BM
	WET / BM
	WET / BM
	WET / BM
	WET / BM

SHOPPING LIST

- ○
- ○
- ○
- ○
- ○

SPECIAL CARE

📅 DATE	# WEEK	⚖ WEIGHT

FEED		
MEALS	AMOUNT	TIME

SLEEP		
FROM	TO	DURATION

ACTIVITIES	
DESCRIPTION	DURATION

DIAPER CHANGES	
TIME	RESULT
	WET / BM
	WET / BM
	WET / BM
	WET / BM
	WET / BM
	WET / BM
	WET / BM
	WET / BM

SHOPPING LIST
◯
◯
◯
◯
◯

SPECIAL CARE

📅 DATE	# WEEK	⚖ WEIGHT

FEED

MEALS	AMOUNT	TIME

SLEEP

FROM	TO	DURATION

ACTIVITIES

DESCRIPTION	DURATION

DIAPER CHANGES

TIME	RESULT
	WET / BM
	WET / BM
	WET / BM
	WET / BM
	WET / BM
	WET / BM
	WET / BM
	WET / BM

SHOPPING LIST

- ◯
- ◯
- ◯
- ◯
- ◯

SPECIAL CARE

📅 DATE	#️⃣ WEEK	⚖️ WEIGHT

FEED

MEALS	AMOUNT	TIME

SLEEP

FROM	TO	DURATION

ACTIVITIES

DESCRIPTION	DURATION

DIAPER CHANGES

TIME	RESULT
	WET / BM
	WET / BM
	WET / BM
	WET / BM
	WET / BM
	WET / BM
	WET / BM
	WET / BM

SHOPPING LIST

- ◯
- ◯
- ◯
- ◯
- ◯

SPECIAL CARE

DATE	# WEEK	⚖ WEIGHT

FEED

MEALS	AMOUNT	TIME

SLEEP

FROM	TO	DURATION

ACTIVITIES

DESCRIPTION	DURATION

DIAPER CHANGES

TIME	RESULT
	WET / BM
	WET / BM
	WET / BM
	WET / BM
	WET / BM
	WET / BM
	WET / BM
	WET / BM

SHOPPING LIST

- ○
- ○
- ○
- ○
- ○

SPECIAL CARE

📅 DATE	#️⃣ WEEK	⚖️ WEIGHT

FEED

MEALS	AMOUNT	TIME

SLEEP

FROM	TO	DURATION

ACTIVITIES

DESCRIPTION	DURATION

DIAPER CHANGES

TIME	RESULT
	WET / BM
	WET / BM
	WET / BM
	WET / BM
	WET / BM
	WET / BM
	WET / BM
	WET / BM

SHOPPING LIST

- ◯
- ◯
- ◯
- ◯
- ◯

SPECIAL CARE

📅 DATE	WEEK	⚖️ WEIGHT

FEED

MEALS	AMOUNT	TIME

SLEEP

FROM	TO	DURATION

ACTIVITIES

DESCRIPTION	DURATION

DIAPER CHANGES

TIME	RESULT
	WET / BM
	WET / BM
	WET / BM
	WET / BM
	WET / BM
	WET / BM
	WET / BM
	WET / BM

SHOPPING LIST

- ○
- ○
- ○
- ○
- ○

SPECIAL CARE

📅 DATE	# WEEK	⚖️ WEIGHT

FEED

MEALS	AMOUNT	TIME

SLEEP

FROM	TO	DURATION

ACTIVITIES

DESCRIPTION	DURATION

DIAPER CHANGES

TIME	RESULT
	WET / BM
	WET / BM
	WET / BM
	WET / BM
	WET / BM
	WET / BM
	WET / BM
	WET / BM

SHOPPING LIST

- ○
- ○
- ○
- ○
- ○

SPECIAL CARE

📅 DATE	# WEEK	⚖ WEIGHT

FEED

MEALS	AMOUNT	TIME

SLEEP

FROM	TO	DURATION

ACTIVITIES

DESCRIPTION	DURATION

DIAPER CHANGES

TIME	RESULT
	WET / BM
	WET / BM
	WET / BM
	WET / BM
	WET / BM
	WET / BM
	WET / BM
	WET / BM

SHOPPING LIST

- ○
- ○
- ○
- ○
- ○

SPECIAL CARE

🗓 DATE	# WEEK	⚖ WEIGHT

FEED

MEALS	AMOUNT	TIME

SLEEP

FROM	TO	DURATION

ACTIVITIES

DESCRIPTION	DURATION

DIAPER CHANGES

TIME	RESULT
	WET / BM
	WET / BM
	WET / BM
	WET / BM
	WET / BM
	WET / BM
	WET / BM
	WET / BM

SHOPPING LIST

- ○
- ○
- ○
- ○
- ○

SPECIAL CARE

📅 DATE	WEEK	⚖️ WEIGHT

FEED

MEALS	AMOUNT	TIME

SLEEP

FROM	TO	DURATION

ACTIVITIES

DESCRIPTION	DURATION

DIAPER CHANGES

TIME	RESULT
	WET / BM
	WET / BM
	WET / BM
	WET / BM
	WET / BM
	WET / BM
	WET / BM
	WET / BM

SHOPPING LIST

- ○
- ○
- ○
- ○
- ○

SPECIAL CARE

📅 DATE	# WEEK	⚖️ WEIGHT

FEED		
MEALS	AMOUNT	TIME

SLEEP		
FROM	TO	DURATION

ACTIVITIES	
DESCRIPTION	DURATION

DIAPER CHANGES	
TIME	RESULT
	WET / BM
	WET / BM
	WET / BM
	WET / BM
	WET / BM
	WET / BM
	WET / BM
	WET / BM

SHOPPING LIST
○
○
○
○
○

SPECIAL CARE

📅 DATE	# WEEK	⚖️ WEIGHT

FEED

MEALS	AMOUNT	TIME

SLEEP

FROM	TO	DURATION

ACTIVITIES

DESCRIPTION	DURATION

DIAPER CHANGES

TIME	RESULT
	WET / BM
	WET / BM
	WET / BM
	WET / BM
	WET / BM
	WET / BM
	WET / BM
	WET / BM

SHOPPING LIST

- ○
- ○
- ○
- ○
- ○

SPECIAL CARE

📅 DATE	#️⃣ WEEK	⚖️ WEIGHT

FEED

MEALS	AMOUNT	TIME

SLEEP

FROM	TO	DURATION

ACTIVITIES

DESCRIPTION	DURATION

DIAPER CHANGES

TIME	RESULT
	WET / BM
	WET / BM
	WET / BM
	WET / BM
	WET / BM
	WET / BM
	WET / BM
	WET / BM

SHOPPING LIST

- ○
- ○
- ○
- ○
- ○

SPECIAL CARE

📅 DATE	# WEEK	⚖️ WEIGHT

FEED

MEALS	AMOUNT	TIME

SLEEP

FROM	TO	DURATION

ACTIVITIES

DESCRIPTION	DURATION

DIAPER CHANGES

TIME	RESULT
	WET / BM
	WET / BM
	WET / BM
	WET / BM
	WET / BM
	WET / BM
	WET / BM
	WET / BM

SHOPPING LIST

- ○
- ○
- ○
- ○
- ○

SPECIAL CARE

📅 DATE	# WEEK	⚖️ WEIGHT

FEED

MEALS	AMOUNT	TIME

SLEEP

FROM	TO	DURATION

ACTIVITIES

DESCRIPTION	DURATION

DIAPER CHANGES

TIME	RESULT
	WET / BM
	WET / BM
	WET / BM
	WET / BM
	WET / BM
	WET / BM
	WET / BM
	WET / BM

SHOPPING LIST

- ○
- ○
- ○
- ○
- ○

SPECIAL CARE

📅 DATE	#️⃣ WEEK	⚖️ WEIGHT

FEED

MEALS	AMOUNT	TIME

SLEEP

FROM	TO	DURATION

ACTIVITIES

DESCRIPTION	DURATION

DIAPER CHANGES

TIME	RESULT
	WET / BM
	WET / BM
	WET / BM
	WET / BM
	WET / BM
	WET / BM
	WET / BM
	WET / BM

SHOPPING LIST

- ○
- ○
- ○
- ○
- ○

SPECIAL CARE

DATE	# WEEK	🔲 WEIGHT

FEED

MEALS	AMOUNT	TIME

SLEEP

FROM	TO	DURATION

ACTIVITIES

DESCRIPTION	DURATION

DIAPER CHANGES

TIME	RESULT
	WET / BM
	WET / BM
	WET / BM
	WET / BM
	WET / BM
	WET / BM
	WET / BM
	WET / BM

SHOPPING LIST

- ◯
- ◯
- ◯
- ◯
- ◯

SPECIAL CARE

📅 DATE	# WEEK	⚖️ WEIGHT

FEED

MEALS	AMOUNT	TIME

SLEEP

FROM	TO	DURATION

ACTIVITIES

DESCRIPTION	DURATION

DIAPER CHANGES

TIME	RESULT
	WET / BM
	WET / BM
	WET / BM
	WET / BM
	WET / BM
	WET / BM
	WET / BM
	WET / BM

SHOPPING LIST

- ○
- ○
- ○
- ○
- ○

SPECIAL CARE

📅 DATE	#️⃣ WEEK	⚖️ WEIGHT

FEED

MEALS	AMOUNT	TIME

SLEEP

FROM	TO	DURATION

ACTIVITIES

DESCRIPTION	DURATION

DIAPER CHANGES

TIME	RESULT
	WET / BM
	WET / BM
	WET / BM
	WET / BM
	WET / BM
	WET / BM
	WET / BM
	WET / BM

SHOPPING LIST

- ◯
- ◯
- ◯
- ◯
- ◯

SPECIAL CARE

📅 DATE	# WEEK	⚖️ WEIGHT

FEED

MEALS	AMOUNT	TIME

SLEEP

FROM	TO	DURATION

ACTIVITIES

DESCRIPTION	DURATION

DIAPER CHANGES

TIME	RESULT
	WET / BM
	WET / BM
	WET / BM
	WET / BM
	WET / BM
	WET / BM
	WET / BM
	WET / BM

SHOPPING LIST

- ○
- ○
- ○
- ○
- ○

SPECIAL CARE

📅 DATE	WEEK	⚖️ WEIGHT

FEED

MEALS	AMOUNT	TIME

SLEEP

FROM	TO	DURATION

ACTIVITIES

DESCRIPTION	DURATION

DIAPER CHANGES

TIME	RESULT
	WET / BM
	WET / BM
	WET / BM
	WET / BM
	WET / BM
	WET / BM
	WET / BM
	WET / BM

SHOPPING LIST

- ◯
- ◯
- ◯
- ◯
- ◯

SPECIAL CARE

📅 DATE	WEEK	⚖️ WEIGHT

FEED

MEALS	AMOUNT	TIME

SLEEP

FROM	TO	DURATION

ACTIVITIES

DESCRIPTION	DURATION

DIAPER CHANGES

TIME	RESULT
	WET / BM
	WET / BM
	WET / BM
	WET / BM
	WET / BM
	WET / BM
	WET / BM
	WET / BM

SHOPPING LIST

- ○
- ○
- ○
- ○
- ○

SPECIAL CARE

📅 DATE	#️⃣ WEEK	⚖️ WEIGHT

FEED

MEALS	AMOUNT	TIME

SLEEP

FROM	TO	DURATION

ACTIVITIES

DESCRIPTION	DURATION

DIAPER CHANGES

TIME	RESULT
	WET / BM
	WET / BM
	WET / BM
	WET / BM
	WET / BM
	WET / BM
	WET / BM
	WET / BM

SHOPPING LIST

- ◯
- ◯
- ◯
- ◯
- ◯

SPECIAL CARE

📅 DATE	#️⃣ WEEK	⚖️ WEIGHT

FEED

MEALS	AMOUNT	TIME

SLEEP

FROM	TO	DURATION

ACTIVITIES

DESCRIPTION	DURATION

DIAPER CHANGES

TIME	RESULT
	WET / BM
	WET / BM
	WET / BM
	WET / BM
	WET / BM
	WET / BM
	WET / BM
	WET / BM

SHOPPING LIST

- ○
- ○
- ○
- ○
- ○

SPECIAL CARE

📅 DATE	#️⃣ WEEK	⚖️ WEIGHT

FEED

MEALS	AMOUNT	TIME

SLEEP

FROM	TO	DURATION

ACTIVITIES

DESCRIPTION	DURATION

DIAPER CHANGES

TIME	RESULT
	WET / BM
	WET / BM
	WET / BM
	WET / BM
	WET / BM
	WET / BM
	WET / BM
	WET / BM

SHOPPING LIST

- ○
- ○
- ○
- ○
- ○

SPECIAL CARE

📅 DATE	# WEEK	⚖️ WEIGHT

FEED

MEALS	AMOUNT	TIME

SLEEP

FROM	TO	DURATION

ACTIVITIES

DESCRIPTION	DURATION

DIAPER CHANGES

TIME	RESULT
	WET / BM
	WET / BM
	WET / BM
	WET / BM
	WET / BM
	WET / BM
	WET / BM
	WET / BM

SHOPPING LIST

- ◯
- ◯
- ◯
- ◯
- ◯

SPECIAL CARE

📅 DATE	# WEEK	⚖️ WEIGHT

FEED		
MEALS	AMOUNT	TIME

SLEEP		
FROM	TO	DURATION

ACTIVITIES	
DESCRIPTION	DURATION

DIAPER CHANGES	
TIME	RESULT
	WET / BM
	WET / BM
	WET / BM
	WET / BM
	WET / BM
	WET / BM
	WET / BM
	WET / BM

SHOPPING LIST
○
○
○
○
○

SPECIAL CARE

📅 DATE	#️⃣ WEEK	⚖️ WEIGHT

FEED

MEALS	AMOUNT	TIME

SLEEP

FROM	TO	DURATION

ACTIVITIES

DESCRIPTION	DURATION

DIAPER CHANGES

TIME	RESULT
	WET / BM
	WET / BM
	WET / BM
	WET / BM
	WET / BM
	WET / BM
	WET / BM
	WET / BM

SHOPPING LIST

- ○
- ○
- ○
- ○
- ○

SPECIAL CARE

📅 DATE	#️⃣ WEEK	⚖️ WEIGHT

FEED

MEALS	AMOUNT	TIME

SLEEP

FROM	TO	DURATION

ACTIVITIES

DESCRIPTION	DURATION

DIAPER CHANGES

TIME	RESULT
	WET / BM
	WET / BM
	WET / BM
	WET / BM
	WET / BM
	WET / BM
	WET / BM
	WET / BM

SHOPPING LIST

- ○
- ○
- ○
- ○
- ○

SPECIAL CARE

📅 DATE	#️⃣ WEEK	⚖️ WEIGHT

FEED

MEALS	AMOUNT	TIME

SLEEP

FROM	TO	DURATION

ACTIVITIES

DESCRIPTION	DURATION

DIAPER CHANGES

TIME	RESULT
	WET / BM
	WET / BM
	WET / BM
	WET / BM
	WET / BM
	WET / BM
	WET / BM
	WET / BM

SHOPPING LIST

- ◯
- ◯
- ◯
- ◯
- ◯

SPECIAL CARE

📅 DATE	# WEEK	⚖ WEIGHT

FEED

MEALS	AMOUNT	TIME

SLEEP

FROM	TO	DURATION

ACTIVITIES

DESCRIPTION	DURATION

DIAPER CHANGES

TIME	RESULT
	WET / BM
	WET / BM
	WET / BM
	WET / BM
	WET / BM
	WET / BM
	WET / BM
	WET / BM

SHOPPING LIST

- ○
- ○
- ○
- ○
- ○

SPECIAL CARE

DATE	# WEEK	⚖ WEIGHT

FEED

MEALS	AMOUNT	TIME

SLEEP

FROM	TO	DURATION

ACTIVITIES

DESCRIPTION	DURATION

DIAPER CHANGES

TIME	RESULT
	WET / BM
	WET / BM
	WET / BM
	WET / BM
	WET / BM
	WET / BM
	WET / BM
	WET / BM

SHOPPING LIST

- ○
- ○
- ○
- ○
- ○

SPECIAL CARE

📅 DATE	#️⃣ WEEK	⚖️ WEIGHT

FEED

MEALS	AMOUNT	TIME

SLEEP

FROM	TO	DURATION

ACTIVITIES

DESCRIPTION	DURATION

DIAPER CHANGES

TIME	RESULT
	WET / BM
	WET / BM
	WET / BM
	WET / BM
	WET / BM
	WET / BM
	WET / BM
	WET / BM

SHOPPING LIST

- ◯
- ◯
- ◯
- ◯
- ◯

SPECIAL CARE

📅 DATE	# WEEK	⚖️ WEIGHT

FEED

MEALS	AMOUNT	TIME

SLEEP

FROM	TO	DURATION

ACTIVITIES

DESCRIPTION	DURATION

DIAPER CHANGES

TIME	RESULT
	WET / BM
	WET / BM
	WET / BM
	WET / BM
	WET / BM
	WET / BM
	WET / BM
	WET / BM

SHOPPING LIST

- ◯
- ◯
- ◯
- ◯
- ◯

SPECIAL CARE

📅 DATE	#️⃣ WEEK	⚖️ WEIGHT

FEED

MEALS	AMOUNT	TIME

SLEEP

FROM	TO	DURATION

ACTIVITIES

DESCRIPTION	DURATION

DIAPER CHANGES

TIME	RESULT
	WET / BM
	WET / BM
	WET / BM
	WET / BM
	WET / BM
	WET / BM
	WET / BM
	WET / BM

SHOPPING LIST

- ◯
- ◯
- ◯
- ◯
- ◯

SPECIAL CARE

📅 DATE	# WEEK	⚖️ WEIGHT

FEED

MEALS	AMOUNT	TIME

SLEEP

FROM	TO	DURATION

ACTIVITIES

DESCRIPTION	DURATION

DIAPER CHANGES

TIME	RESULT
	WET / BM
	WET / BM
	WET / BM
	WET / BM
	WET / BM
	WET / BM
	WET / BM
	WET / BM

SHOPPING LIST

- ◯
- ◯
- ◯
- ◯
- ◯

SPECIAL CARE

DATE	WEEK	WEIGHT

FEED

MEALS	AMOUNT	TIME

SLEEP

FROM	TO	DURATION

ACTIVITIES

DESCRIPTION	DURATION

DIAPER CHANGES

TIME	RESULT
	WET / BM
	WET / BM
	WET / BM
	WET / BM
	WET / BM
	WET / BM
	WET / BM
	WET / BM

SHOPPING LIST

- ◯
- ◯
- ◯
- ◯
- ◯

SPECIAL CARE

	DATE		WEEK		WEIGHT

FEED

MEALS	AMOUNT	TIME

SLEEP

FROM	TO	DURATION

ACTIVITIES

DESCRIPTION	DURATION

DIAPER CHANGES

TIME	RESULT
	WET / BM
	WET / BM
	WET / BM
	WET / BM
	WET / BM
	WET / BM
	WET / BM
	WET / BM

SHOPPING LIST

- ◯
- ◯
- ◯
- ◯
- ◯

SPECIAL CARE

📅 DATE	#️⃣ WEEK	⚖️ WEIGHT

FEED

MEALS	AMOUNT	TIME

SLEEP

FROM	TO	DURATION

ACTIVITIES

DESCRIPTION	DURATION

DIAPER CHANGES

TIME	RESULT
	WET / BM
	WET / BM
	WET / BM
	WET / BM
	WET / BM
	WET / BM
	WET / BM
	WET / BM

SHOPPING LIST

- ○
- ○
- ○
- ○
- ○

SPECIAL CARE

📅 DATE	# WEEK	⚖️ WEIGHT

FEED

MEALS	AMOUNT	TIME

SLEEP

FROM	TO	DURATION

ACTIVITIES

DESCRIPTION	DURATION

DIAPER CHANGES

TIME	RESULT
	WET / BM
	WET / BM
	WET / BM
	WET / BM
	WET / BM
	WET / BM
	WET / BM
	WET / BM

SHOPPING LIST

- ○
- ○
- ○
- ○
- ○

SPECIAL CARE

📅 DATE	#️⃣ WEEK	⚖️ WEIGHT

FEED

MEALS	AMOUNT	TIME

SLEEP

FROM	TO	DURATION

ACTIVITIES

DESCRIPTION	DURATION

DIAPER CHANGES

TIME	RESULT
	WET / BM
	WET / BM
	WET / BM
	WET / BM
	WET / BM
	WET / BM
	WET / BM
	WET / BM

SHOPPING LIST

- ◯
- ◯
- ◯
- ◯
- ◯

SPECIAL CARE

📅 DATE	# WEEK	⚖ WEIGHT

FEED

MEALS	AMOUNT	TIME

SLEEP

FROM	TO	DURATION

ACTIVITIES

DESCRIPTION	DURATION

DIAPER CHANGES

TIME	RESULT
	WET / BM
	WET / BM
	WET / BM
	WET / BM
	WET / BM
	WET / BM
	WET / BM
	WET / BM

SHOPPING LIST

- ◯
- ◯
- ◯
- ◯
- ◯

SPECIAL CARE

📅 DATE	#️⃣ WEEK	⚖️ WEIGHT

FEED

MEALS	AMOUNT	TIME

SLEEP

FROM	TO	DURATION

ACTIVITIES

DESCRIPTION	DURATION

DIAPER CHANGES

TIME	RESULT
	WET / BM
	WET / BM
	WET / BM
	WET / BM
	WET / BM
	WET / BM
	WET / BM
	WET / BM

SHOPPING LIST

- ◯
- ◯
- ◯
- ◯
- ◯

SPECIAL CARE

📅 DATE	# WEEK	⚖️ WEIGHT

FEED

MEALS	AMOUNT	TIME

SLEEP

FROM	TO	DURATION

ACTIVITIES

DESCRIPTION	DURATION

DIAPER CHANGES

TIME	RESULT
	WET / BM
	WET / BM
	WET / BM
	WET / BM
	WET / BM
	WET / BM
	WET / BM
	WET / BM

SHOPPING LIST

- ◯
- ◯
- ◯
- ◯
- ◯

SPECIAL CARE

📅 DATE	#️⃣ WEEK	⚖️ WEIGHT

FEED

MEALS	AMOUNT	TIME

SLEEP

FROM	TO	DURATION

ACTIVITIES

DESCRIPTION	DURATION

DIAPER CHANGES

TIME	RESULT
	WET / BM
	WET / BM
	WET / BM
	WET / BM
	WET / BM
	WET / BM
	WET / BM
	WET / BM

SHOPPING LIST

- ◯
- ◯
- ◯
- ◯
- ◯

SPECIAL CARE

📅 DATE	# WEEK	⚖ WEIGHT

FEED

MEALS	AMOUNT	TIME

SLEEP

FROM	TO	DURATION

ACTIVITIES

DESCRIPTION	DURATION

DIAPER CHANGES

TIME	RESULT
	WET / BM
	WET / BM
	WET / BM
	WET / BM
	WET / BM
	WET / BM
	WET / BM
	WET / BM

SHOPPING LIST

- ◯
- ◯
- ◯
- ◯
- ◯

SPECIAL CARE

📅 DATE	# WEEK	⚖️ WEIGHT

FEED

MEALS	AMOUNT	TIME

SLEEP

FROM	TO	DURATION

ACTIVITIES

DESCRIPTION	DURATION

DIAPER CHANGES

TIME	RESULT
	WET / BM
	WET / BM
	WET / BM
	WET / BM
	WET / BM
	WET / BM
	WET / BM
	WET / BM

SHOPPING LIST

- ○
- ○
- ○
- ○
- ○

SPECIAL CARE

📅 DATE	WEEK	⚖️ WEIGHT

FEED

MEALS	AMOUNT	TIME

SLEEP

FROM	TO	DURATION

ACTIVITIES

DESCRIPTION	DURATION

DIAPER CHANGES

TIME	RESULT
	WET / BM
	WET / BM
	WET / BM
	WET / BM
	WET / BM
	WET / BM
	WET / BM
	WET / BM

SHOPPING LIST

- ○
- ○
- ○
- ○
- ○

SPECIAL CARE

📅 DATE	# WEEK	⚖️ WEIGHT

FEED

MEALS	AMOUNT	TIME

SLEEP

FROM	TO	DURATION

ACTIVITIES

DESCRIPTION	DURATION

DIAPER CHANGES

TIME	RESULT
	WET / BM
	WET / BM
	WET / BM
	WET / BM
	WET / BM
	WET / BM
	WET / BM
	WET / BM

SHOPPING LIST

- ○
- ○
- ○
- ○
- ○

SPECIAL CARE

📅 DATE	# WEEK	⚖️ WEIGHT

FEED

MEALS	AMOUNT	TIME

SLEEP

FROM	TO	DURATION

ACTIVITIES

DESCRIPTION	DURATION

DIAPER CHANGES

TIME	RESULT
	WET / BM
	WET / BM
	WET / BM
	WET / BM
	WET / BM
	WET / BM
	WET / BM
	WET / BM

SHOPPING LIST

- ◯
- ◯
- ◯
- ◯
- ◯

SPECIAL CARE

📅 DATE	#️⃣ WEEK	⚖️ WEIGHT

FEED

MEALS	AMOUNT	TIME

SLEEP

FROM	TO	DURATION

ACTIVITIES

DESCRIPTION	DURATION

DIAPER CHANGES

TIME	RESULT
	WET / BM
	WET / BM
	WET / BM
	WET / BM
	WET / BM
	WET / BM
	WET / BM
	WET / BM

SHOPPING LIST

- ◯
- ◯
- ◯
- ◯
- ◯

SPECIAL CARE

DATE	# WEEK	WEIGHT

FEED

MEALS	AMOUNT	TIME

SLEEP

FROM	TO	DURATION

ACTIVITIES

DESCRIPTION	DURATION

DIAPER CHANGES

TIME	RESULT
	WET / BM
	WET / BM
	WET / BM
	WET / BM
	WET / BM
	WET / BM
	WET / BM
	WET / BM

SHOPPING LIST

- ◯
- ◯
- ◯
- ◯
- ◯

SPECIAL CARE

📅 DATE	#️⃣ WEEK	⚖️ WEIGHT

FEED

MEALS	AMOUNT	TIME

SLEEP

FROM	TO	DURATION

ACTIVITIES

DESCRIPTION	DURATION

DIAPER CHANGES

TIME	RESULT
	WET / BM
	WET / BM
	WET / BM
	WET / BM
	WET / BM
	WET / BM
	WET / BM
	WET / BM

SHOPPING LIST

- ○
- ○
- ○
- ○
- ○

SPECIAL CARE

📅 DATE	WEEK	⚖ WEIGHT

FEED

MEALS	AMOUNT	TIME

SLEEP

FROM	TO	DURATION

ACTIVITIES

DESCRIPTION	DURATION

DIAPER CHANGES

TIME	RESULT
	WET / BM
	WET / BM
	WET / BM
	WET / BM
	WET / BM
	WET / BM
	WET / BM
	WET / BM

SHOPPING LIST

- ○
- ○
- ○
- ○
- ○

SPECIAL CARE